The Bird of Imagining

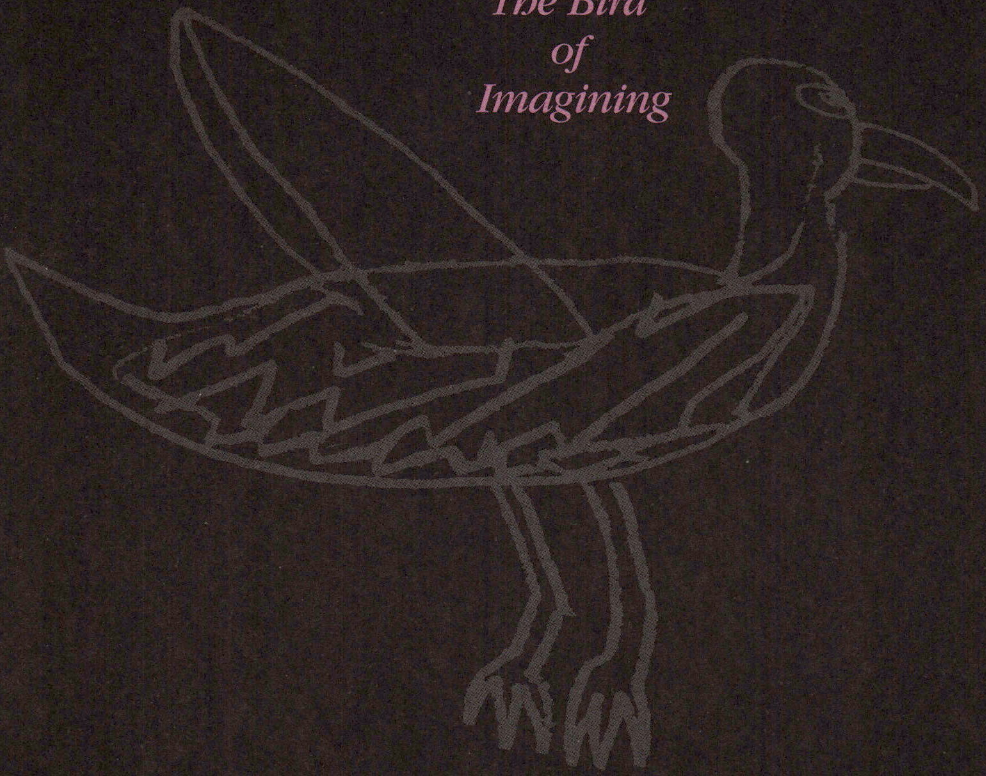

The Bird of Imagining
by Richard Lewis

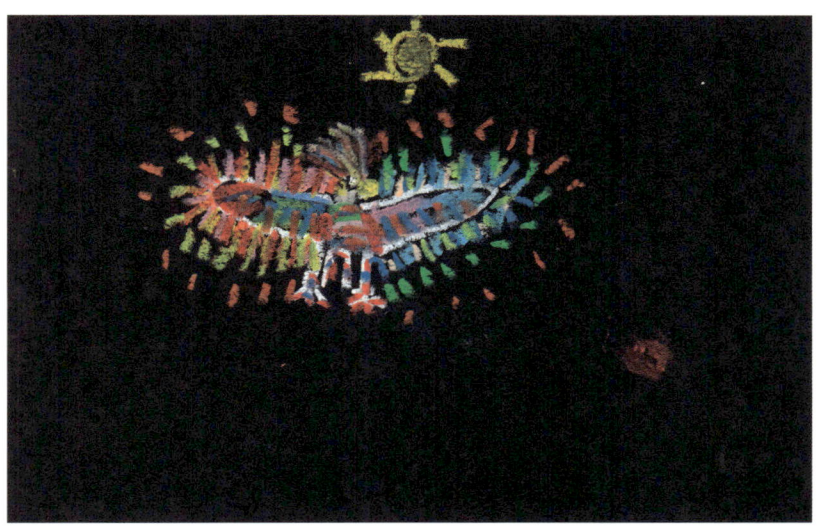

*Drawings by Children
from
New York City Public Schools*

For those of you, child and adult alike, who will not let the life of your imagining disappear.

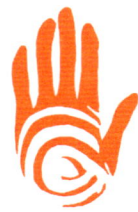

Text, Copyright © 2001 by Richard Lewis
Illustrations, Copyright © 2001 by
The Touchstone Center for Children, Inc.
Library of Congress Control Number: 2001 131664
ISBN: 1-929299-01-X

Design by Martin Moskof

All rights reserved. No part of this book may be reproduced or transmitted in any form or by any means, electronic or mechanical, including photocopying, recording, or by any information storage and retrieval system, without permission in writing from the Publisher.

Touchstone Center Publications
141 East 88th Street • New York NY 10128
Tel: 212-831-7717 • Fax: 212-427-9644
rlewis212@aol.com
www.touchstonecenter.net

To The Reader

What if, inside each one of us, there was a bird? No, not the usual kind of bird, but a bird of imagining. What if this bird had lived a long time in us – and was as old as the most ancient trees still living on the earth? Of course you might wonder what this bird can do, what it looks like, and how it became this special kind of bird.

When I first realized there was a bird of imagining in myself, I wrote a poem about it. I shared the poem with the children I taught – and asked them, after they heard the poem, to draw and write what they thought their bird of imagining looked like.

Soon, with so many different kinds of birds coming to my attention, I decided to choose some of the drawings children had shared with me and, along with my poem, make a book, so that others, like yourself, might find their own birds of imagining.

I hope, as you discover this most noble of birds, it will always fly with you. May it sing of your experience – and the very life of your thoughts and feelings. May it bring you to new and unexpected worlds. May it be the voice of your remembering – and the stirrings of your future.

—R.L.

There was a bird no one had ever seen before.
A bird whose feathers caught the colors
of light shining through them,
so that each feather
reflected the hues of all the days
and all the nights.

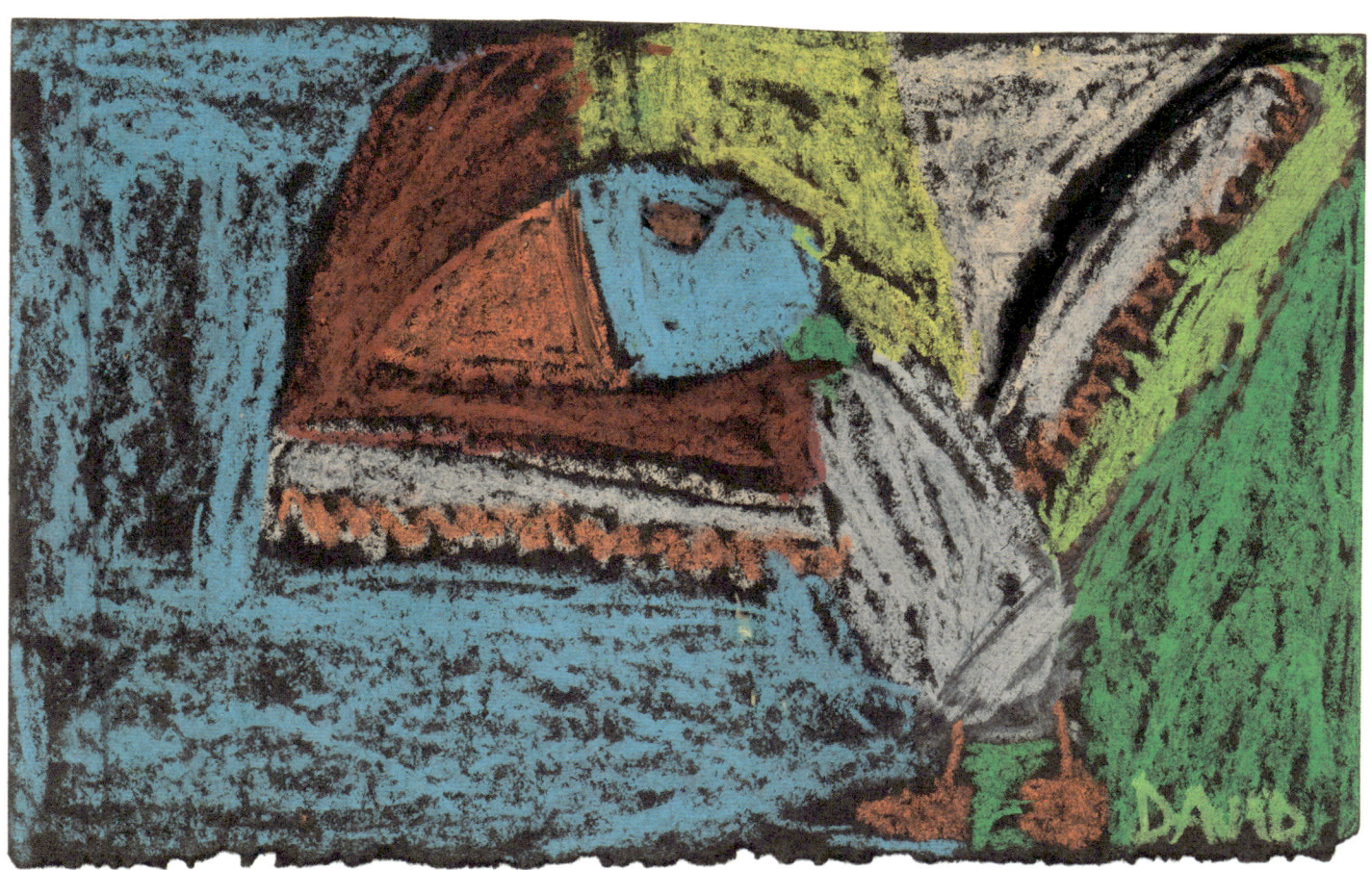

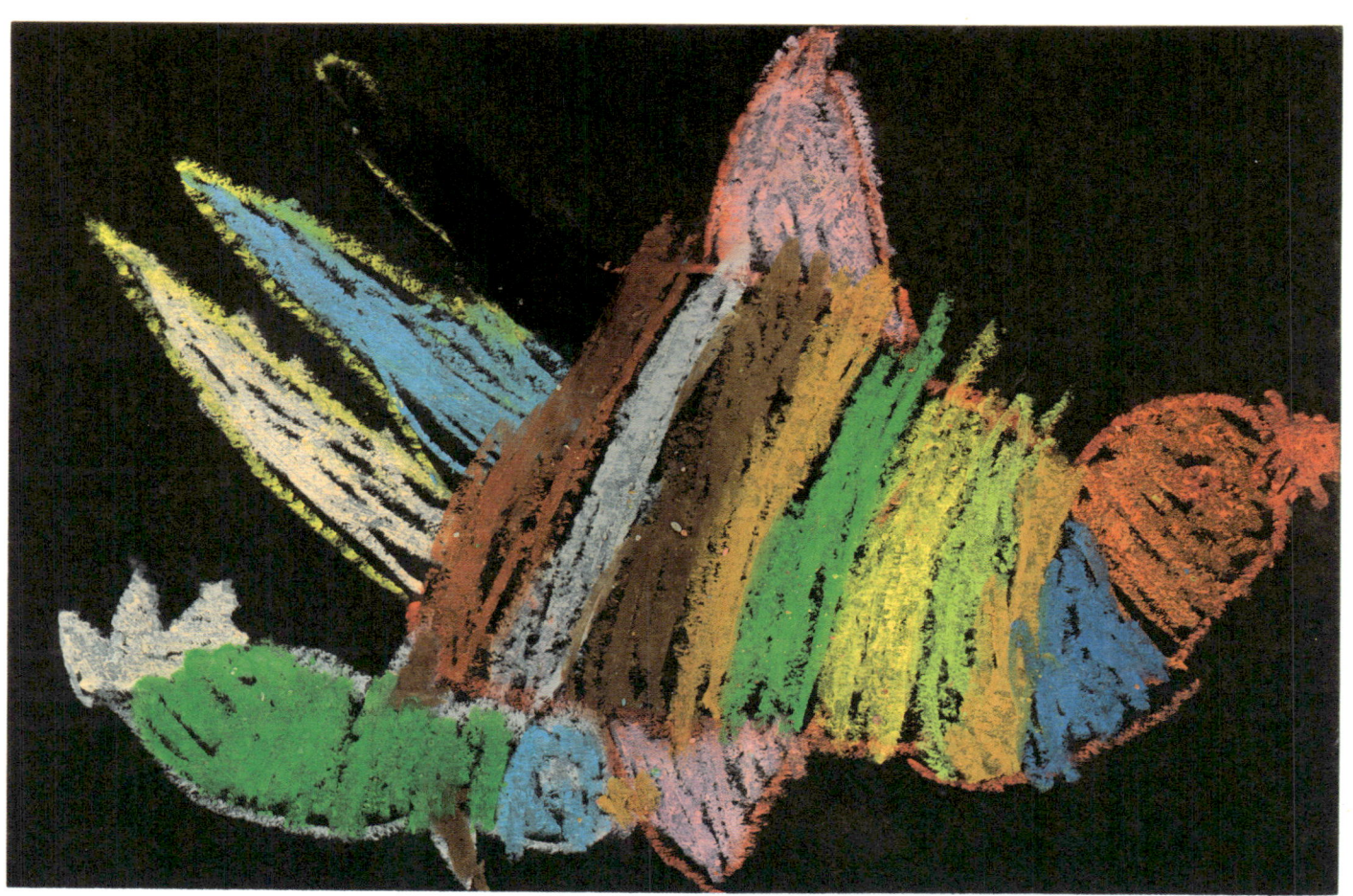

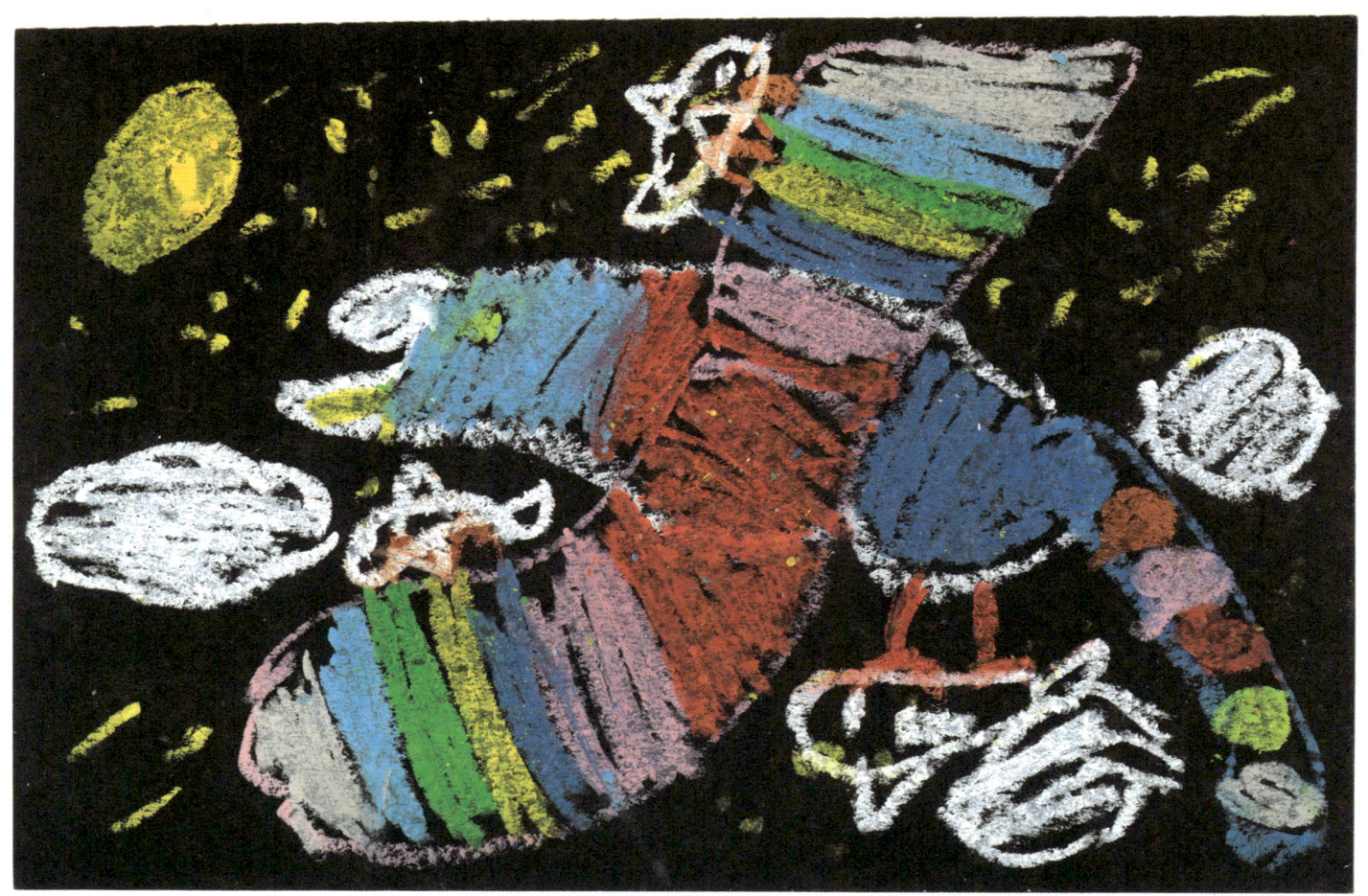

There was a bird no one had ever seen before.
A bird whose eyes could feel the time
of what had been and what will be –
and feeling the life of all this time,
could see inside and outside of what it saw.

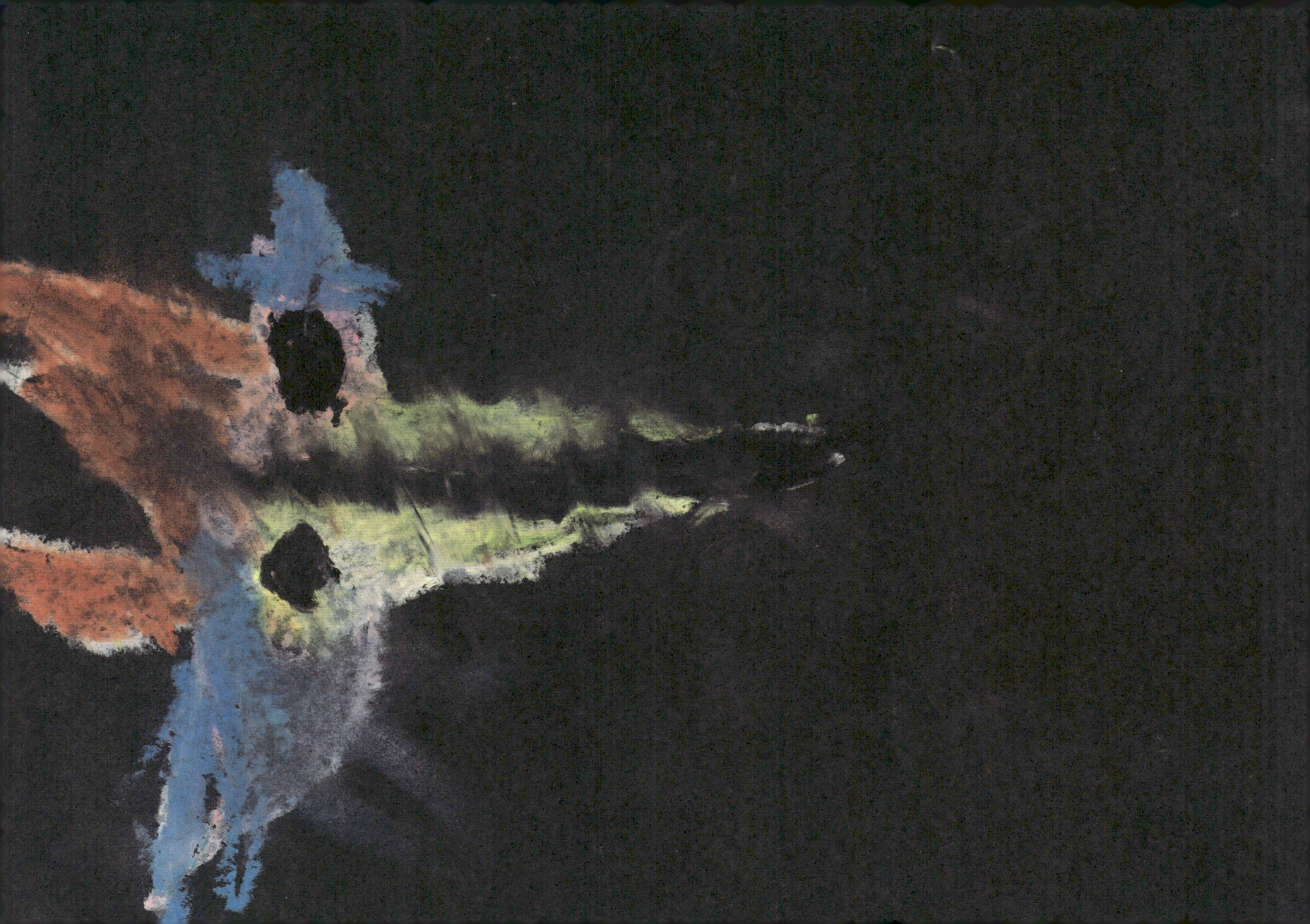

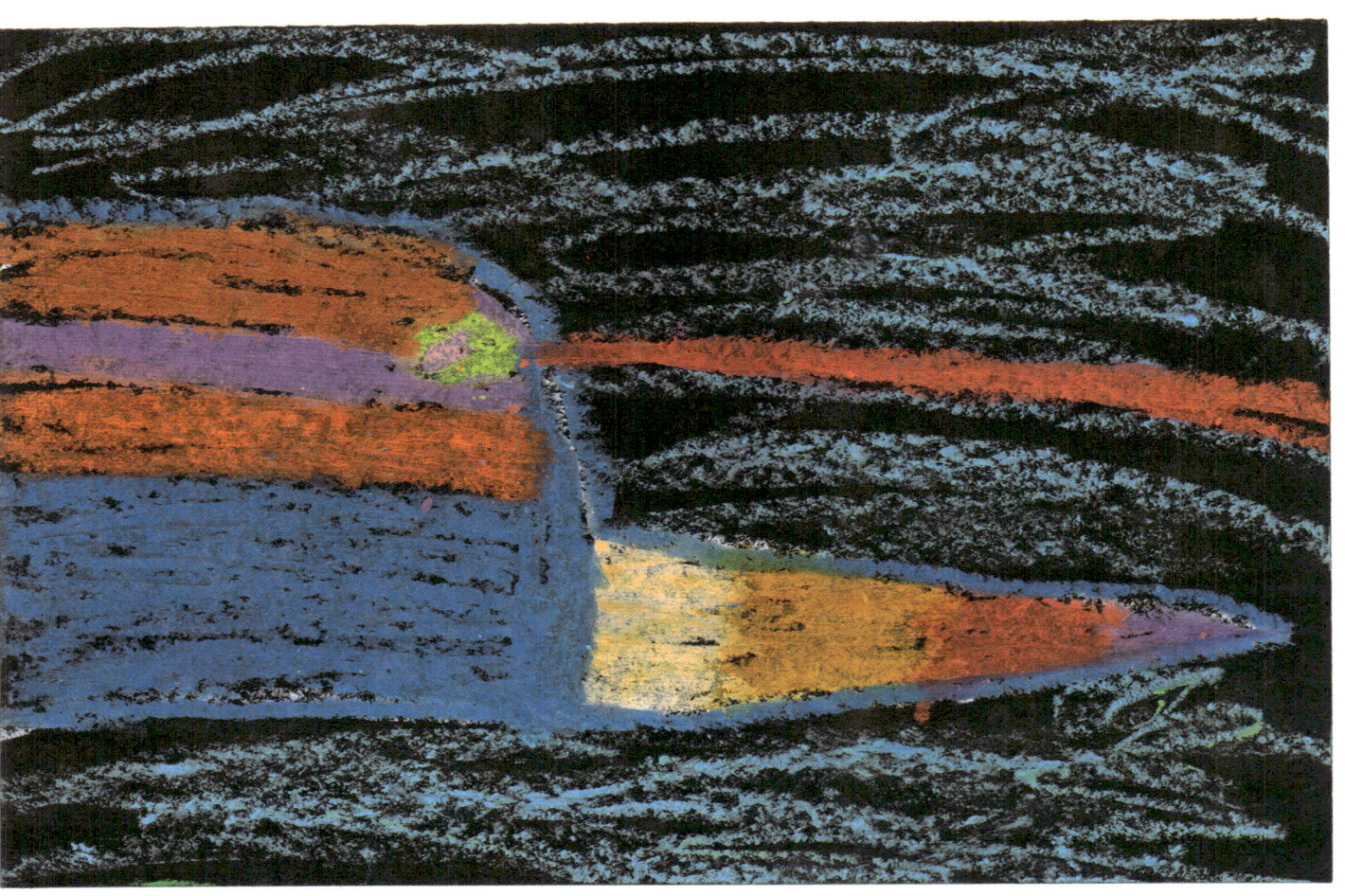

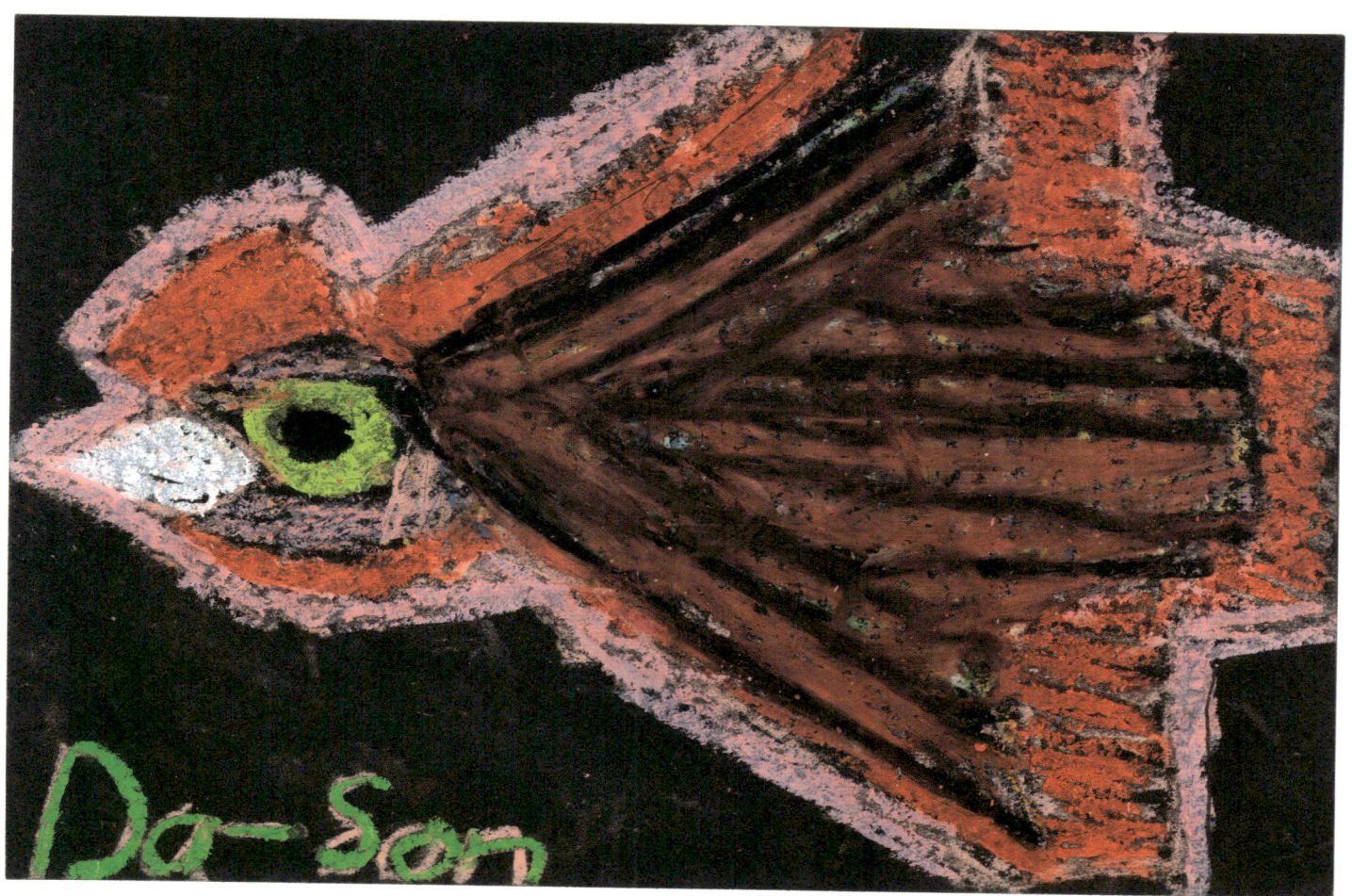

There was a bird no one had ever seen before.
A bird whose wings gathered the air around them,
filling the weight of those wings with the breathing of
    creatures,
listening, in suspense, to other sounds.

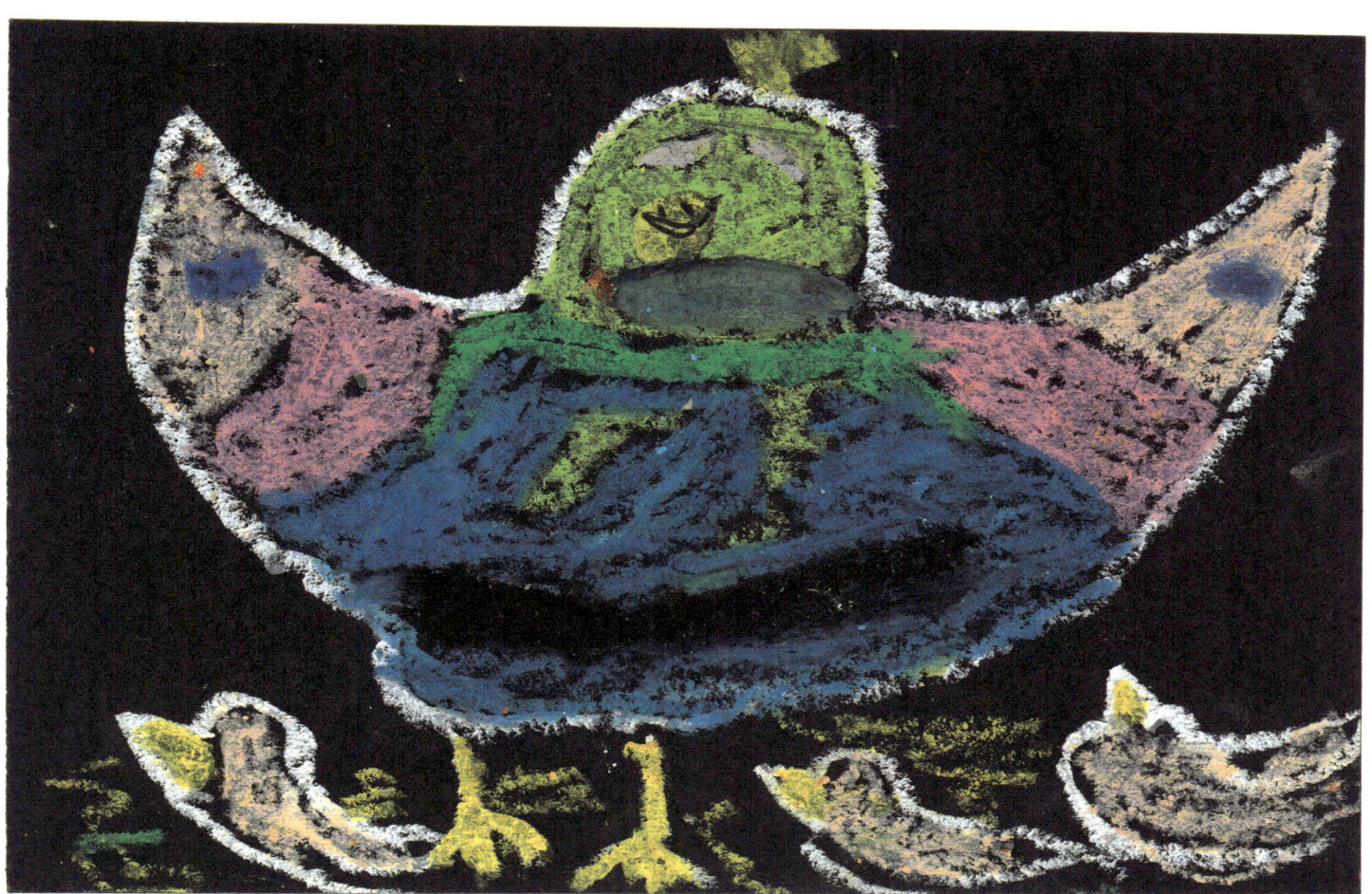

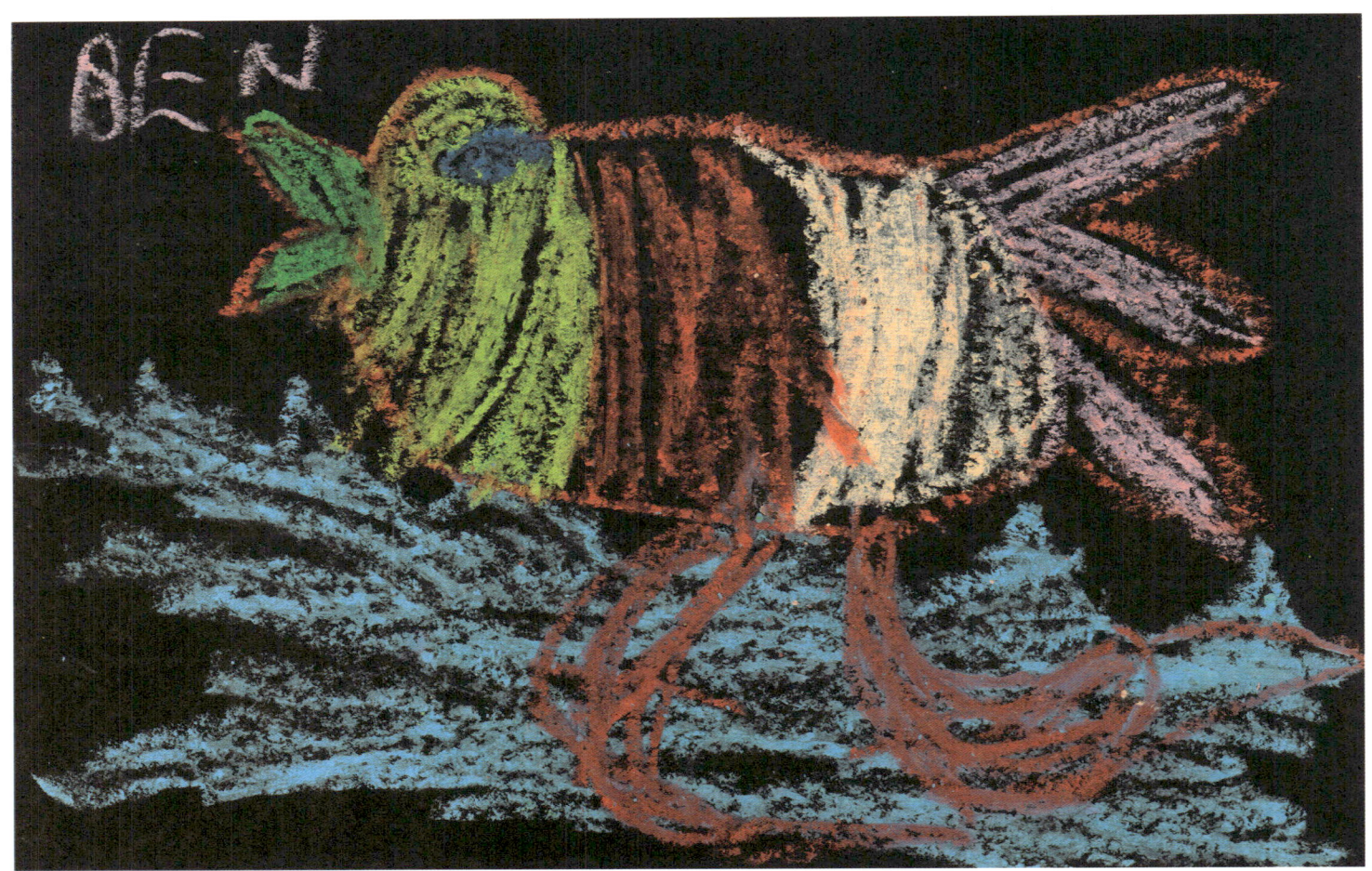

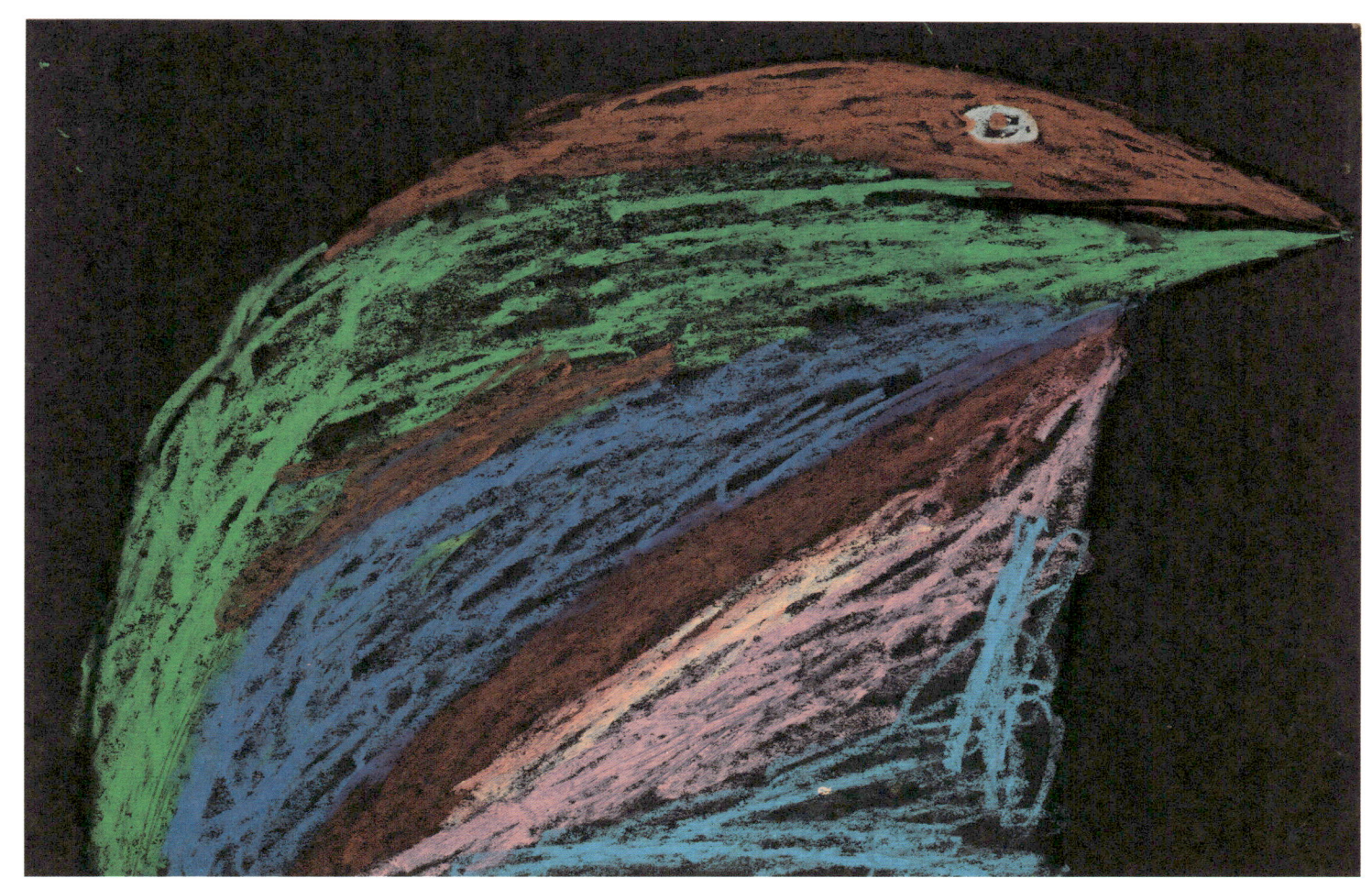

There was a bird no one had ever seen before.
A bird whose voices were the words of dreams,
changing into the songs that brought the stars closer,
so they could have the warmth of their singing nearby.

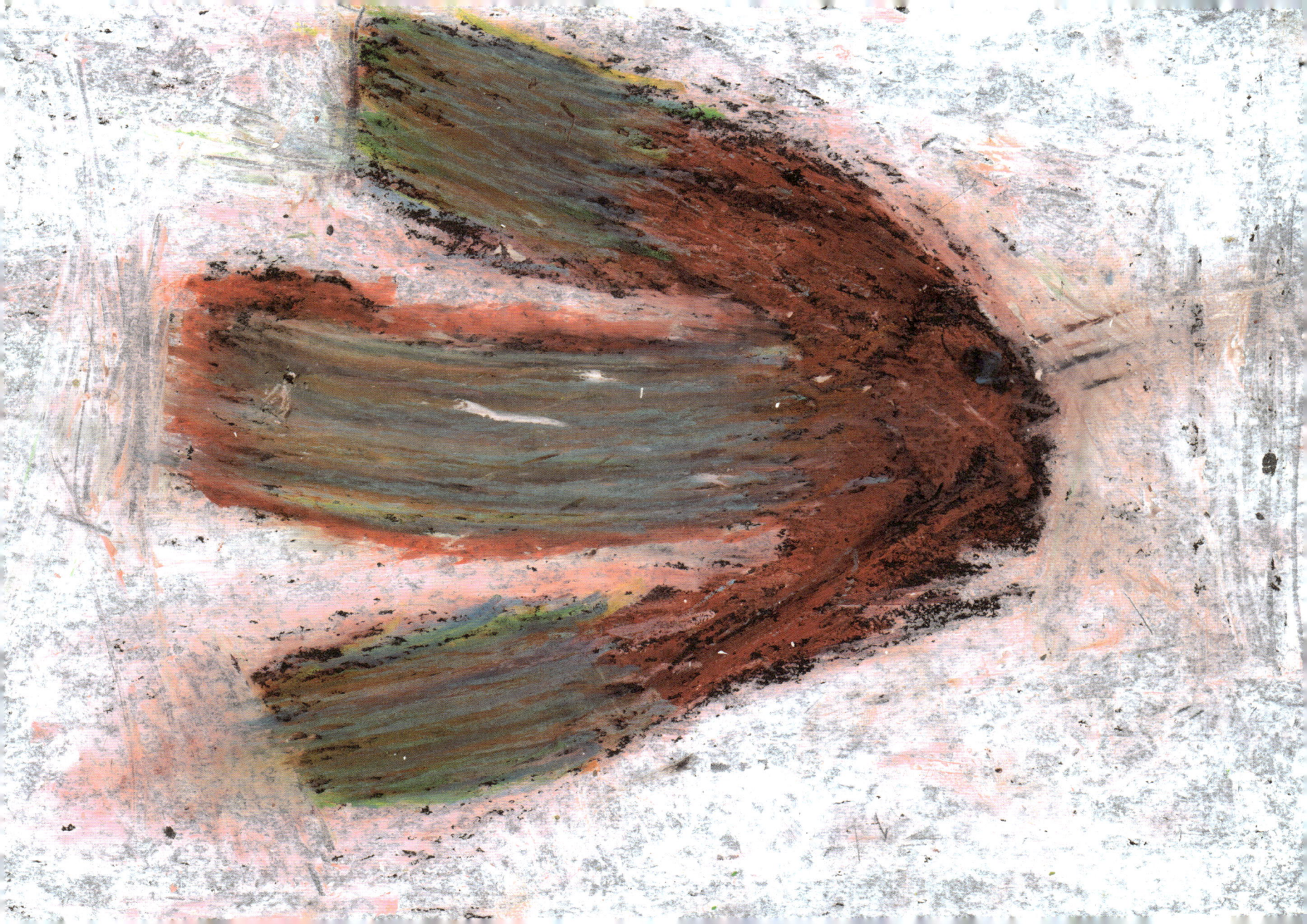

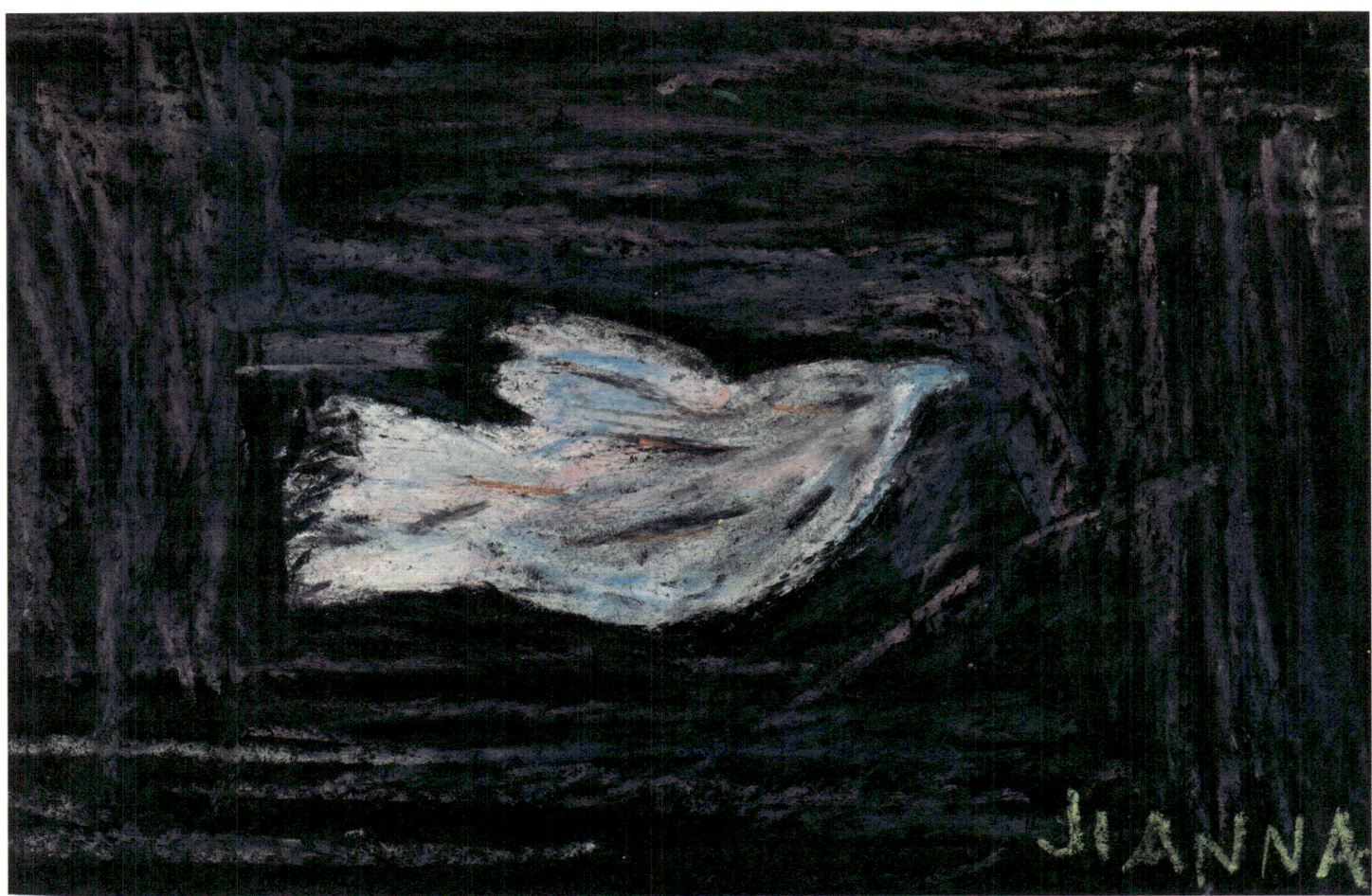

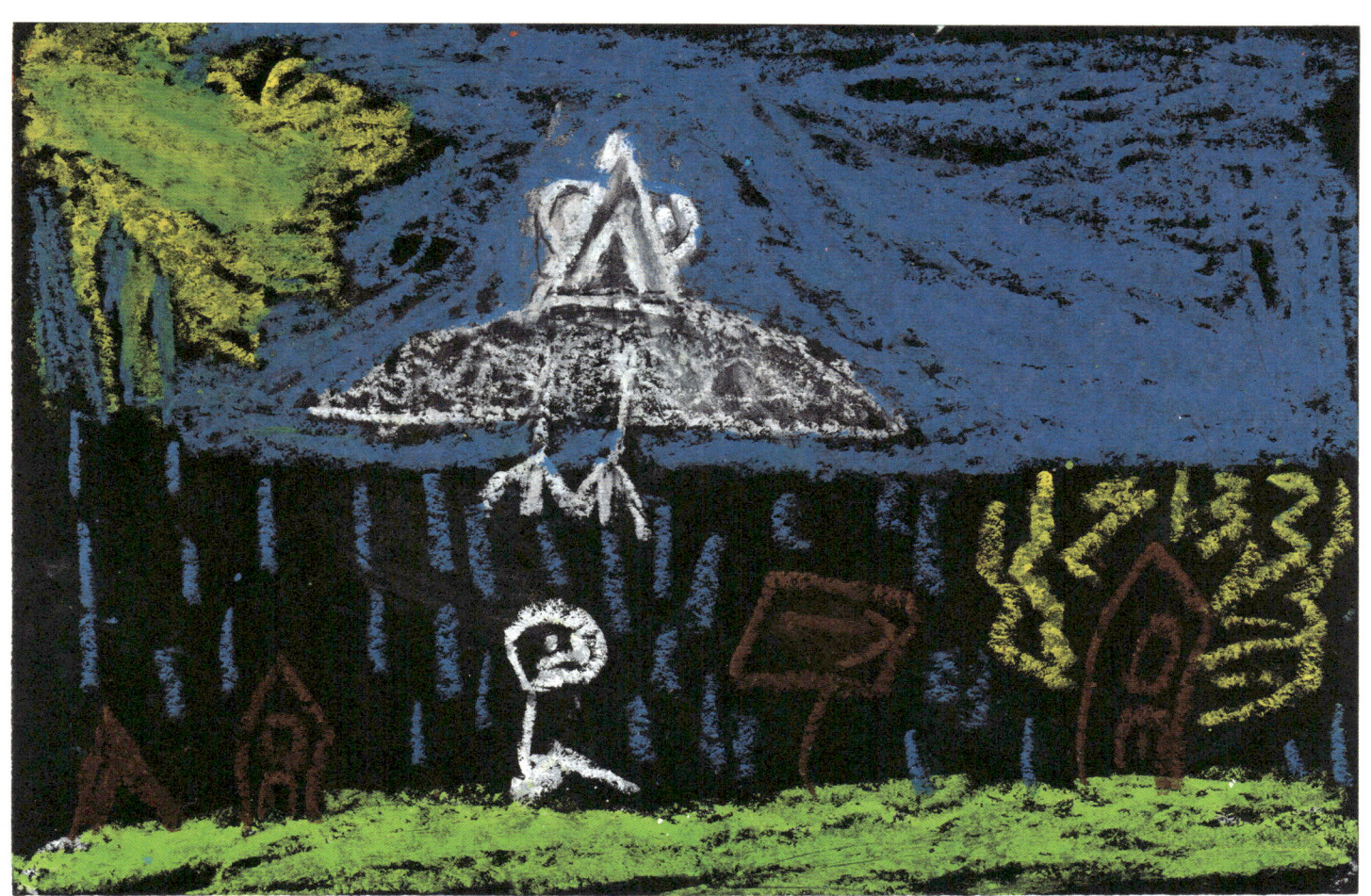

There was a bird no one had ever seen before,
and it was – *ourselves*,

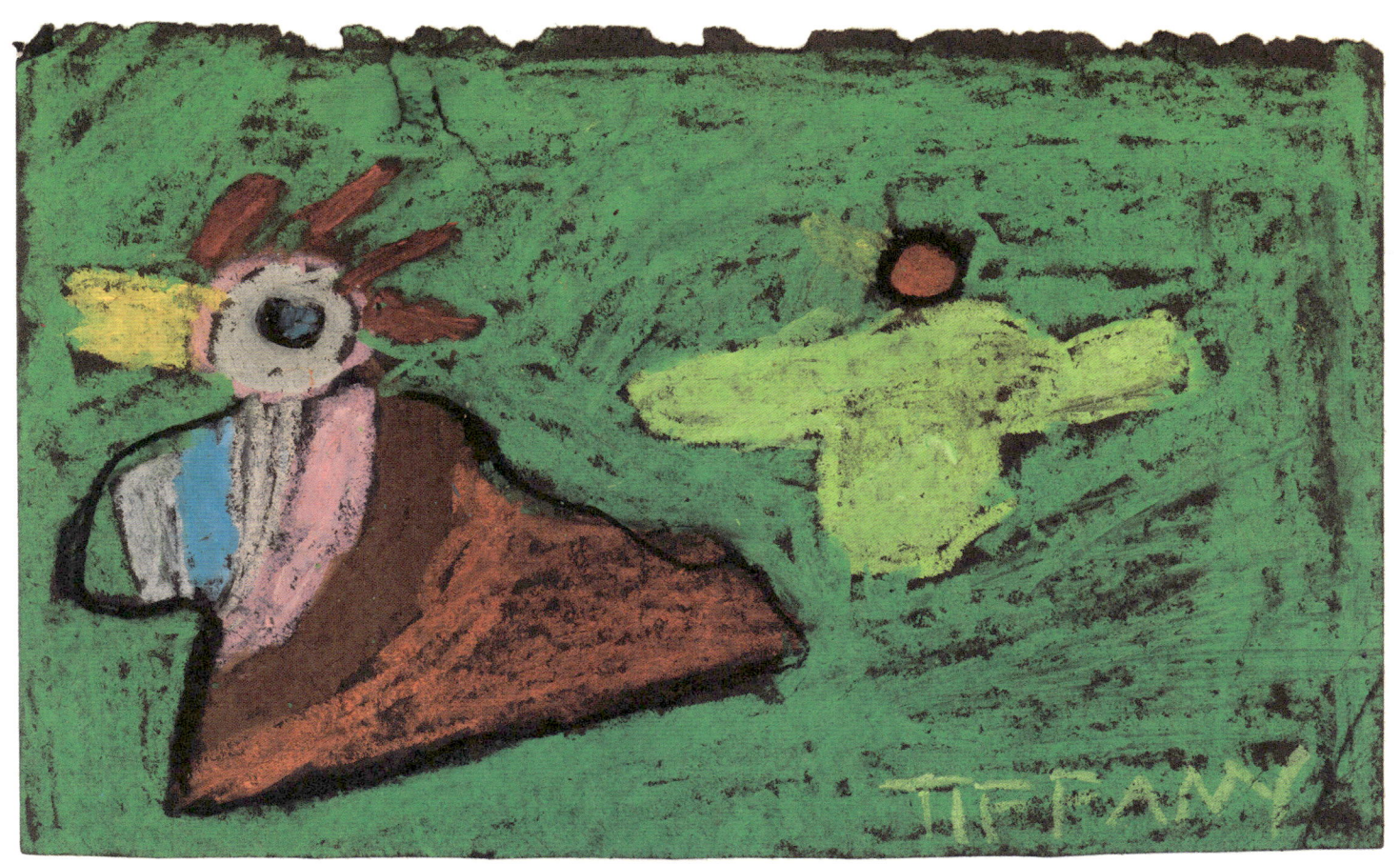

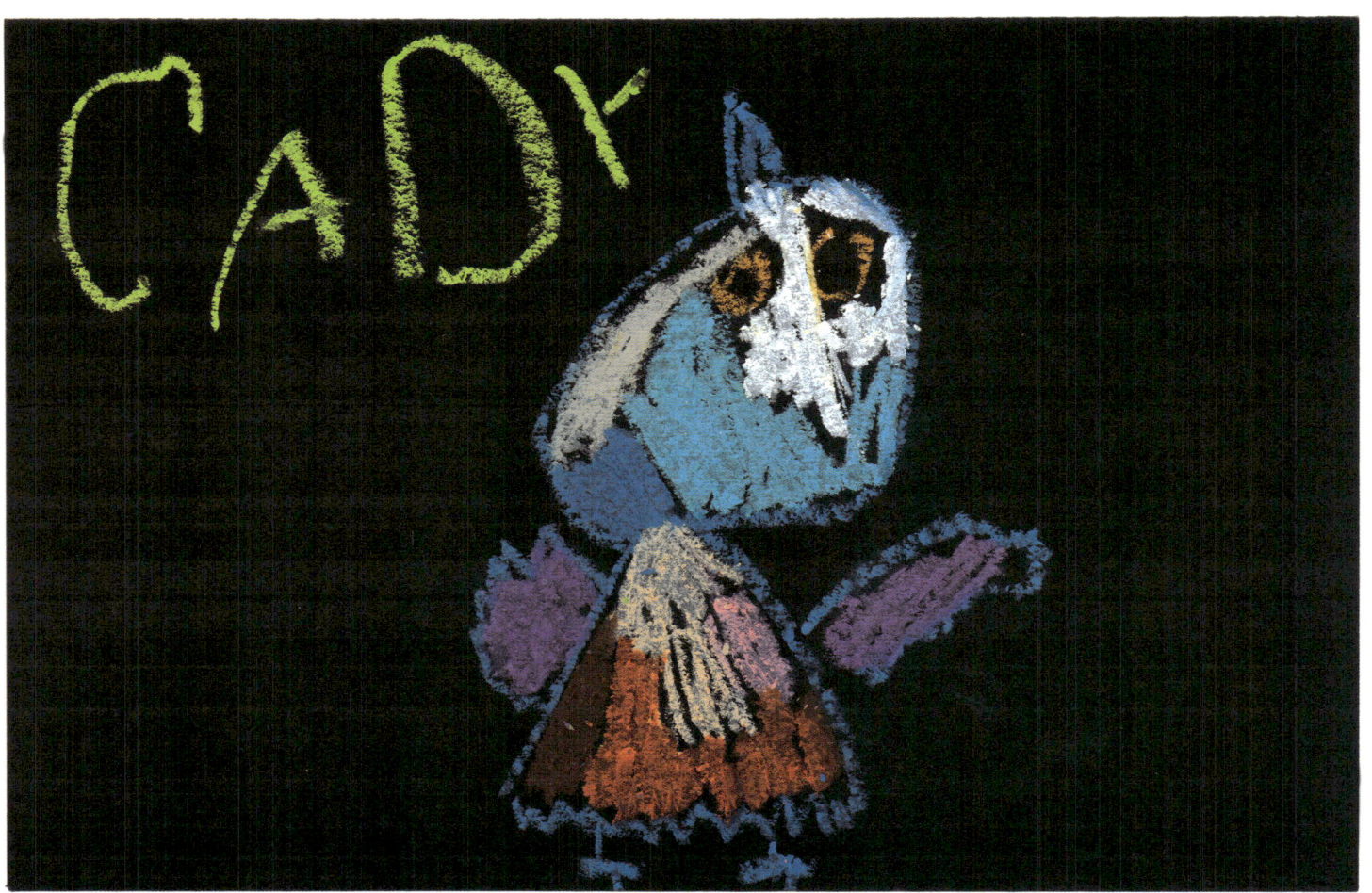

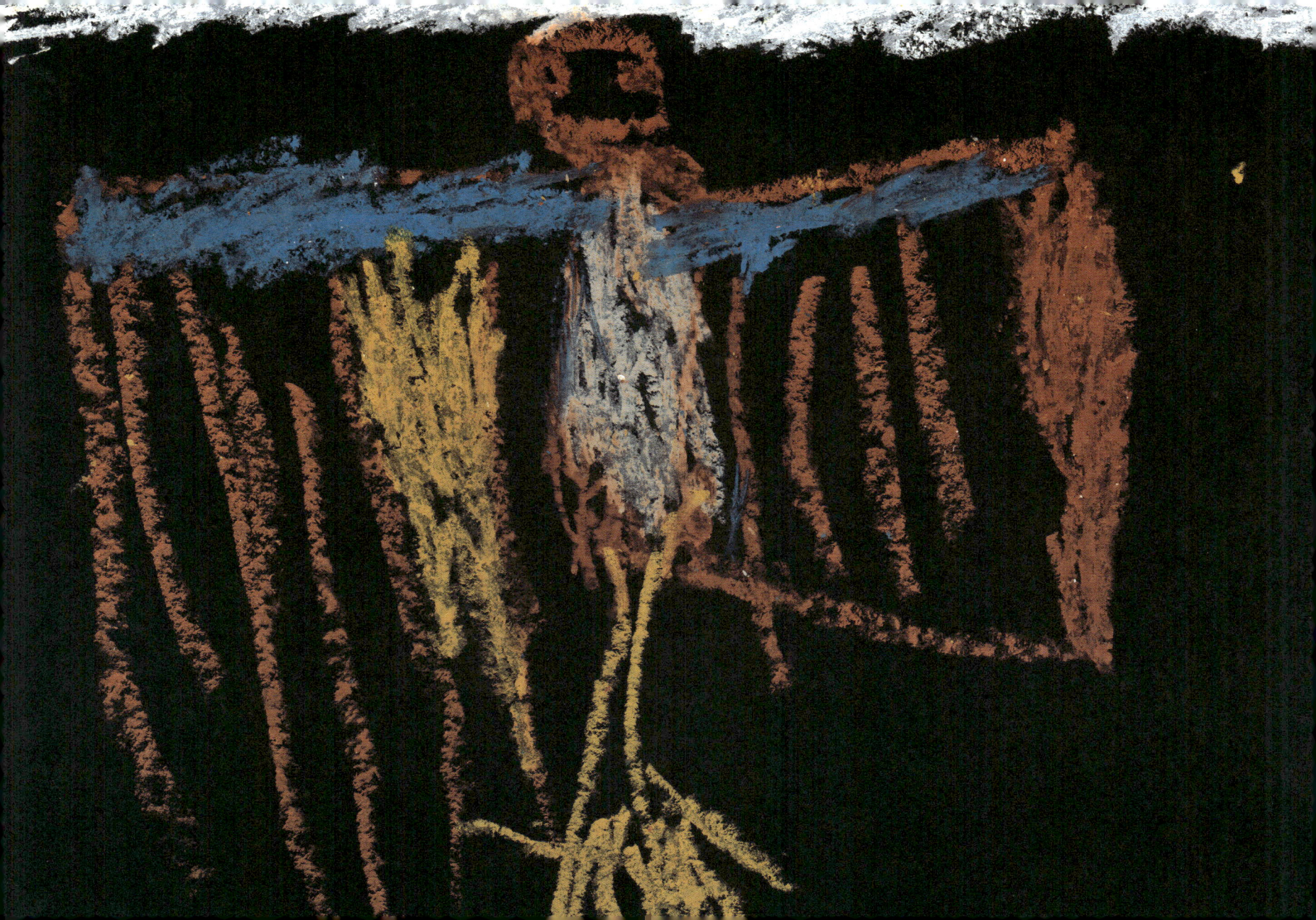

ready to be in the sky of our thoughts,
to be the dreaming of our night into day,

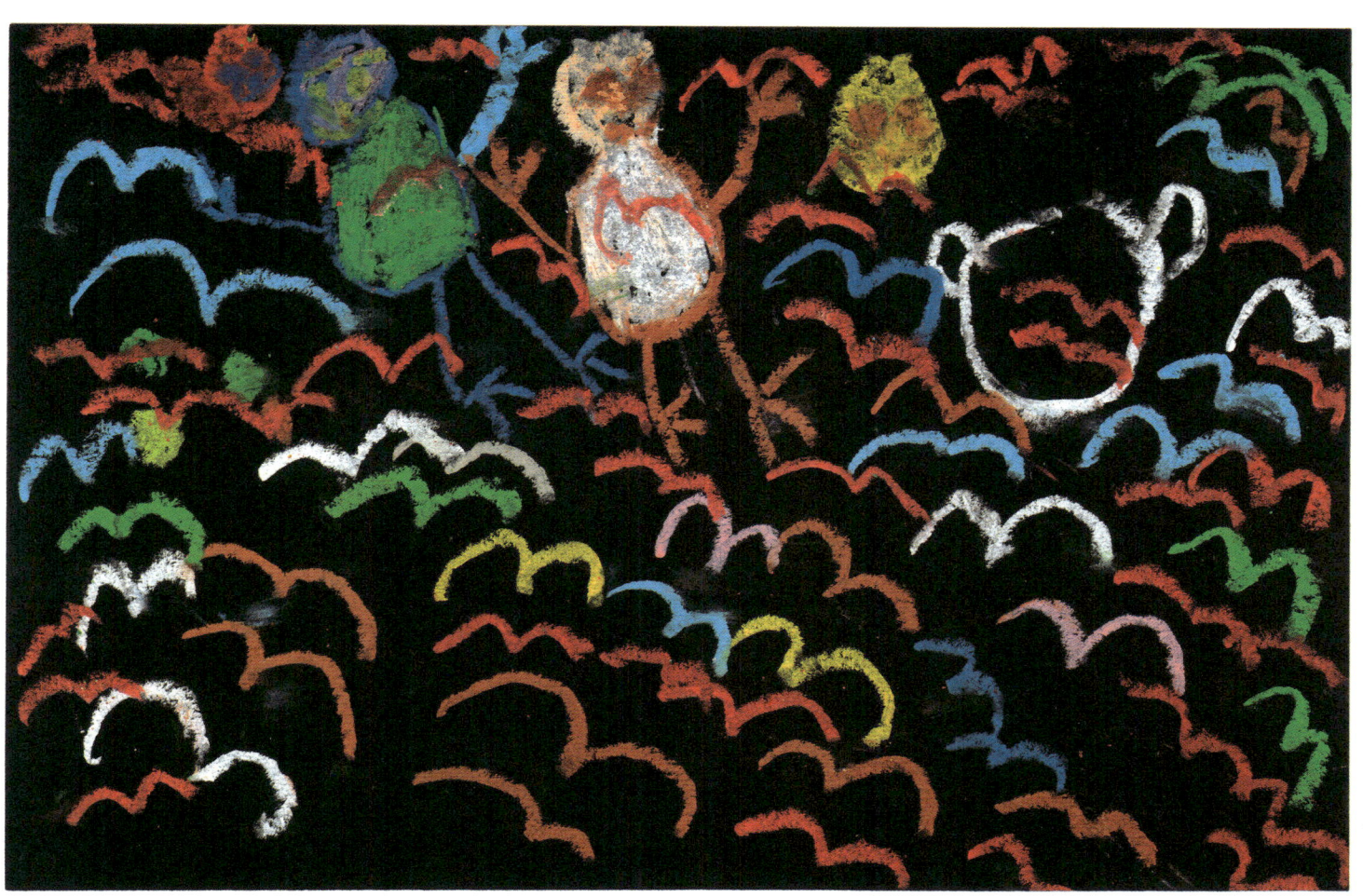

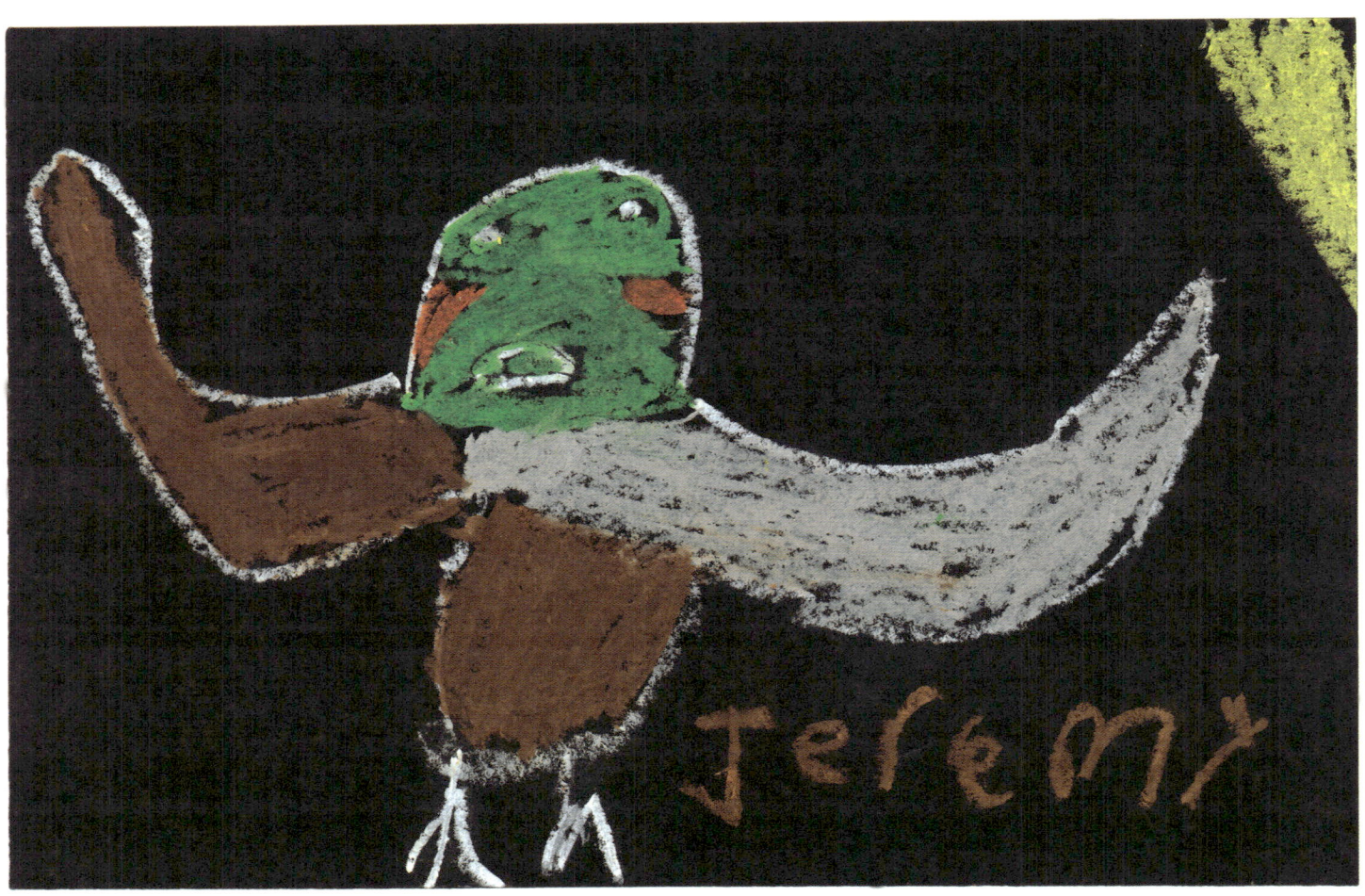

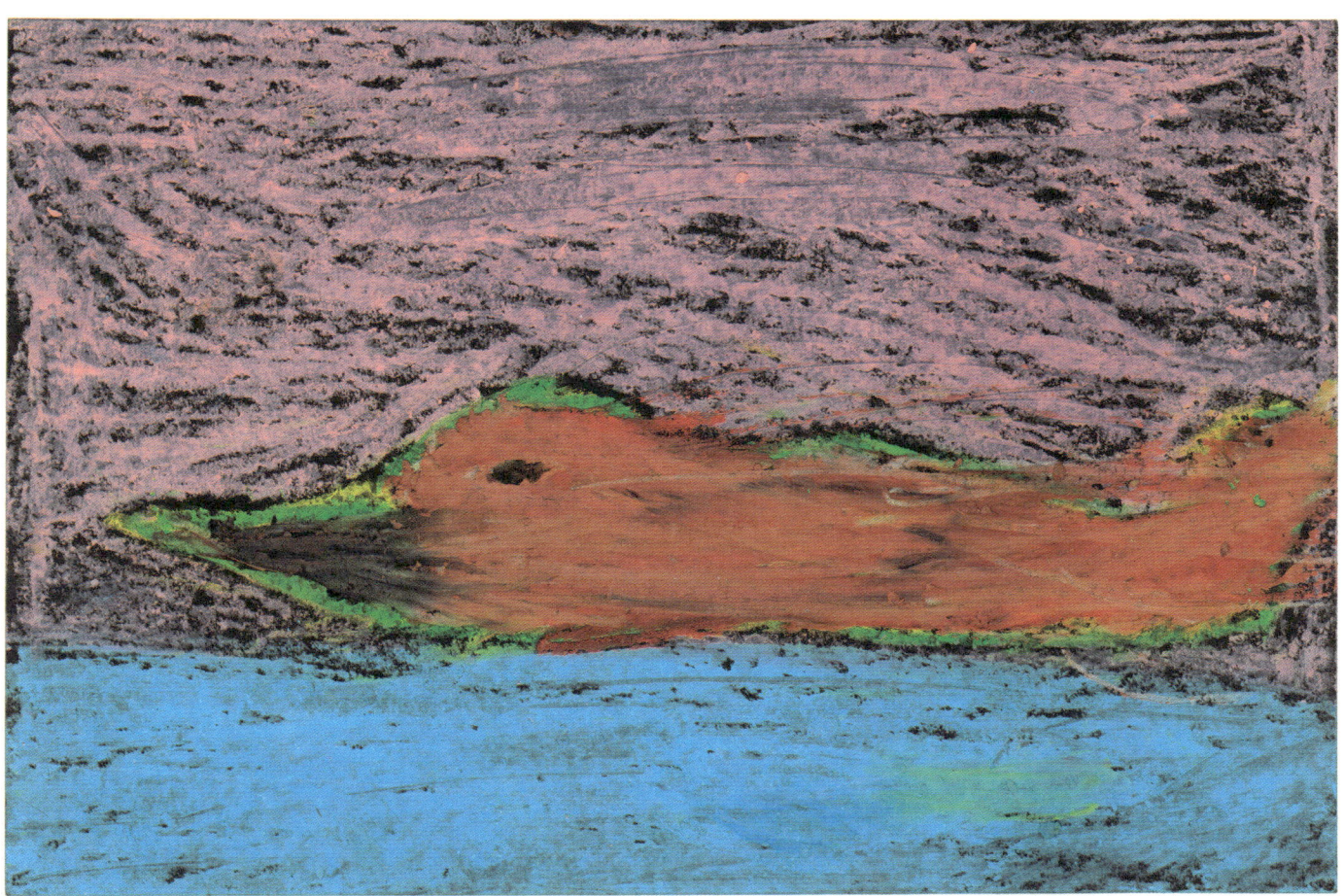

to be the speaking of our words into song,
to be the feet of our dance,
to be the music of our play.

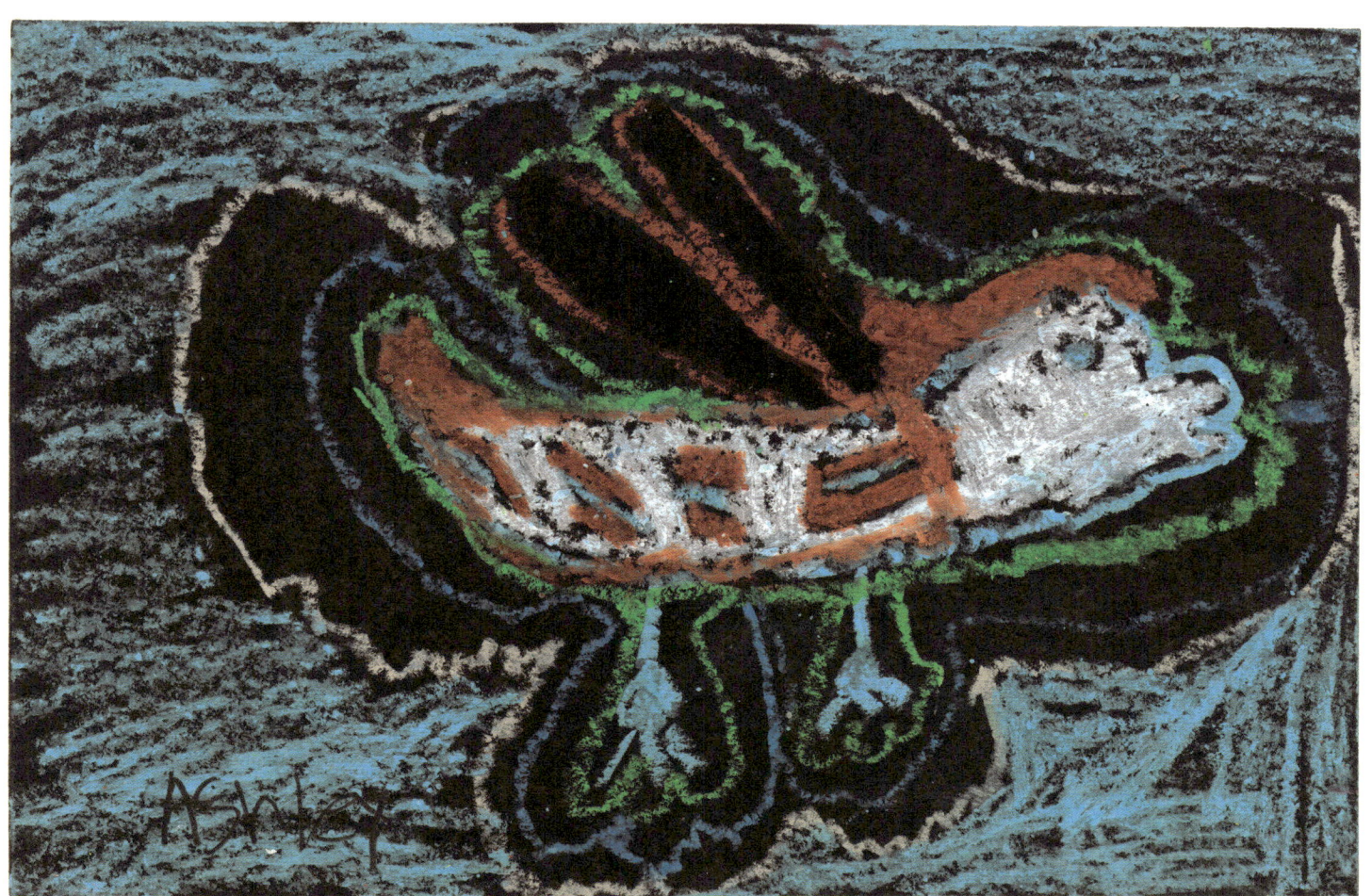

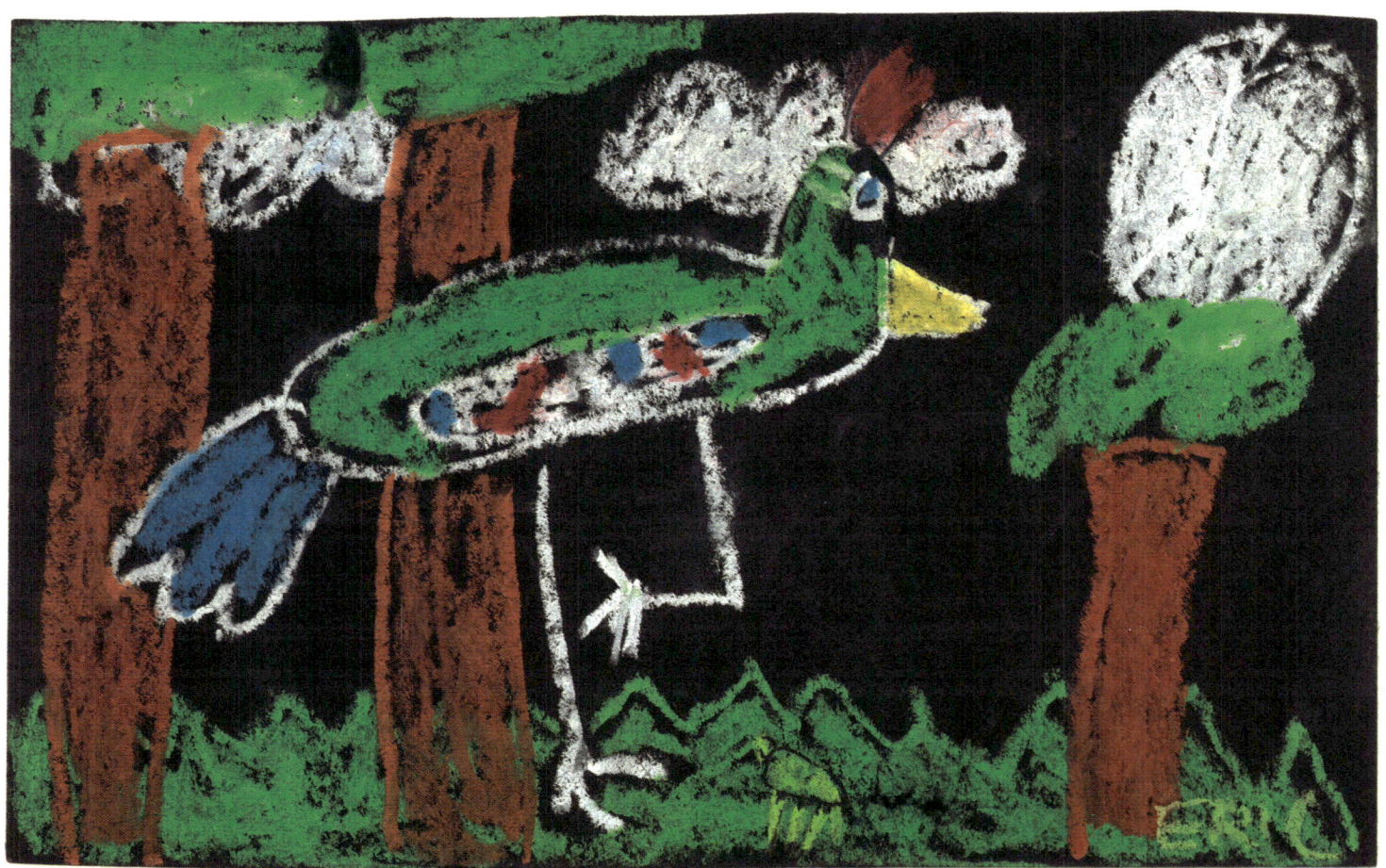

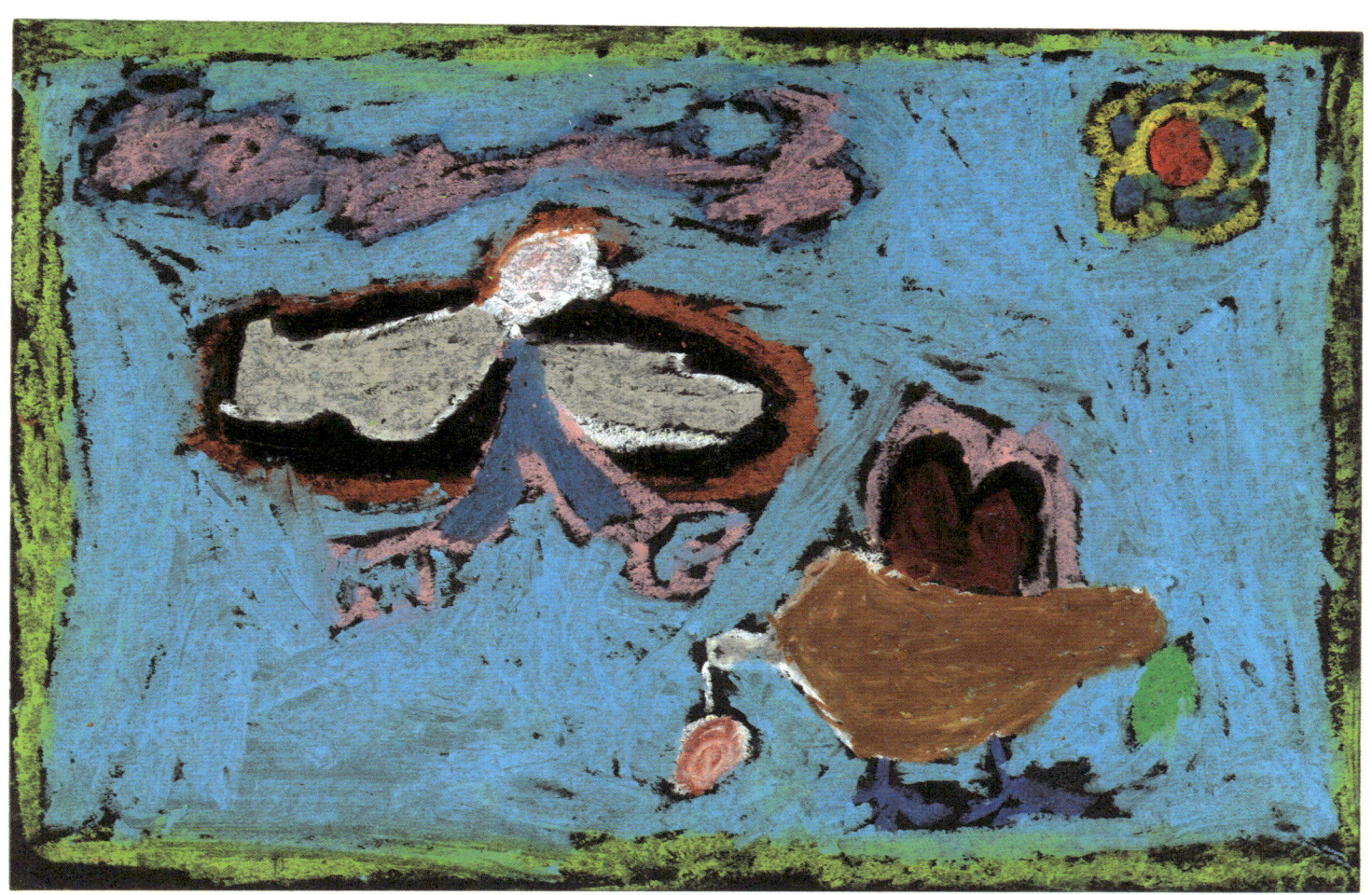

There was a bird no one had ever seen before,

and it flew –

and nothing,

and no one,

was ever the same afterwards . . .

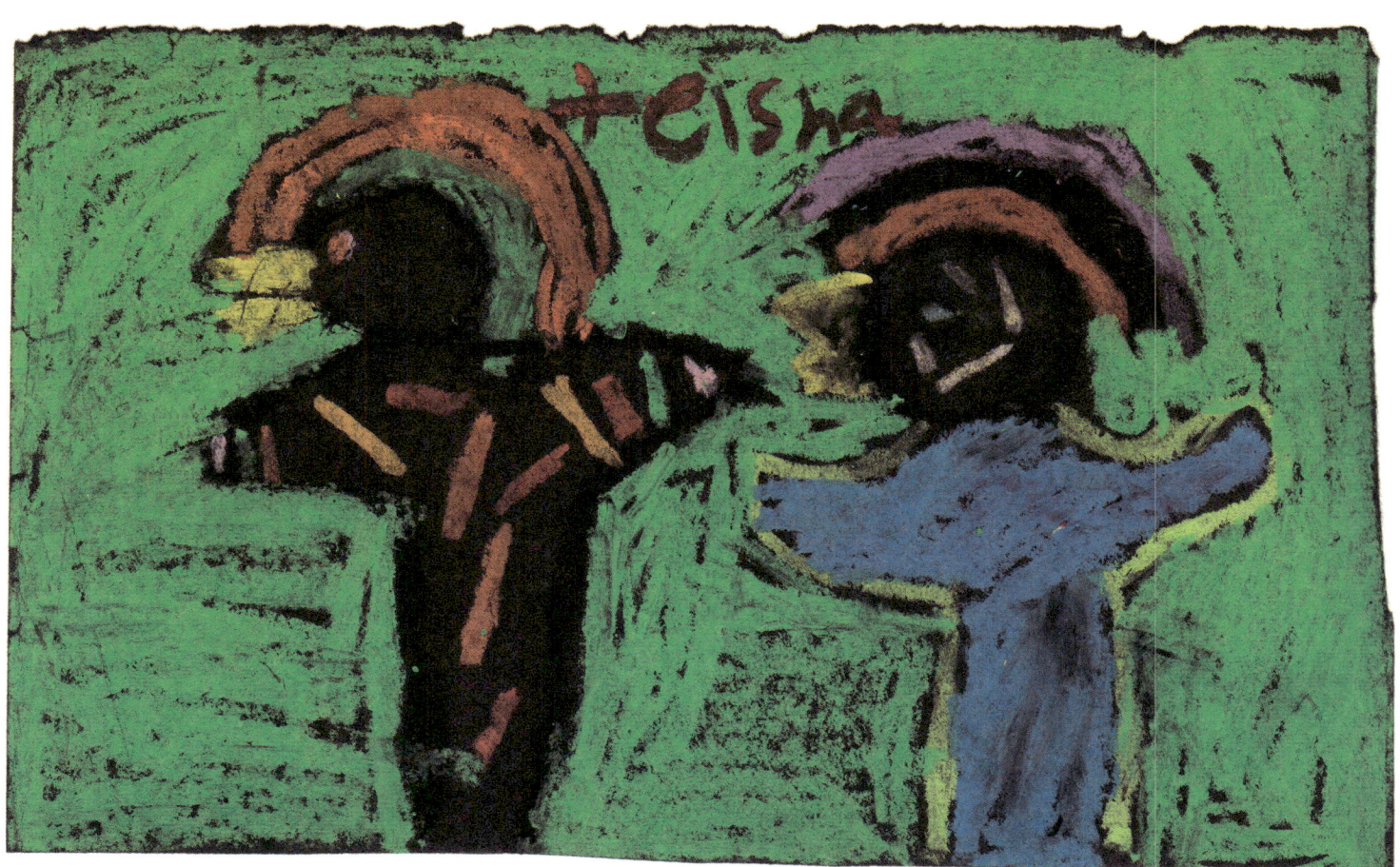

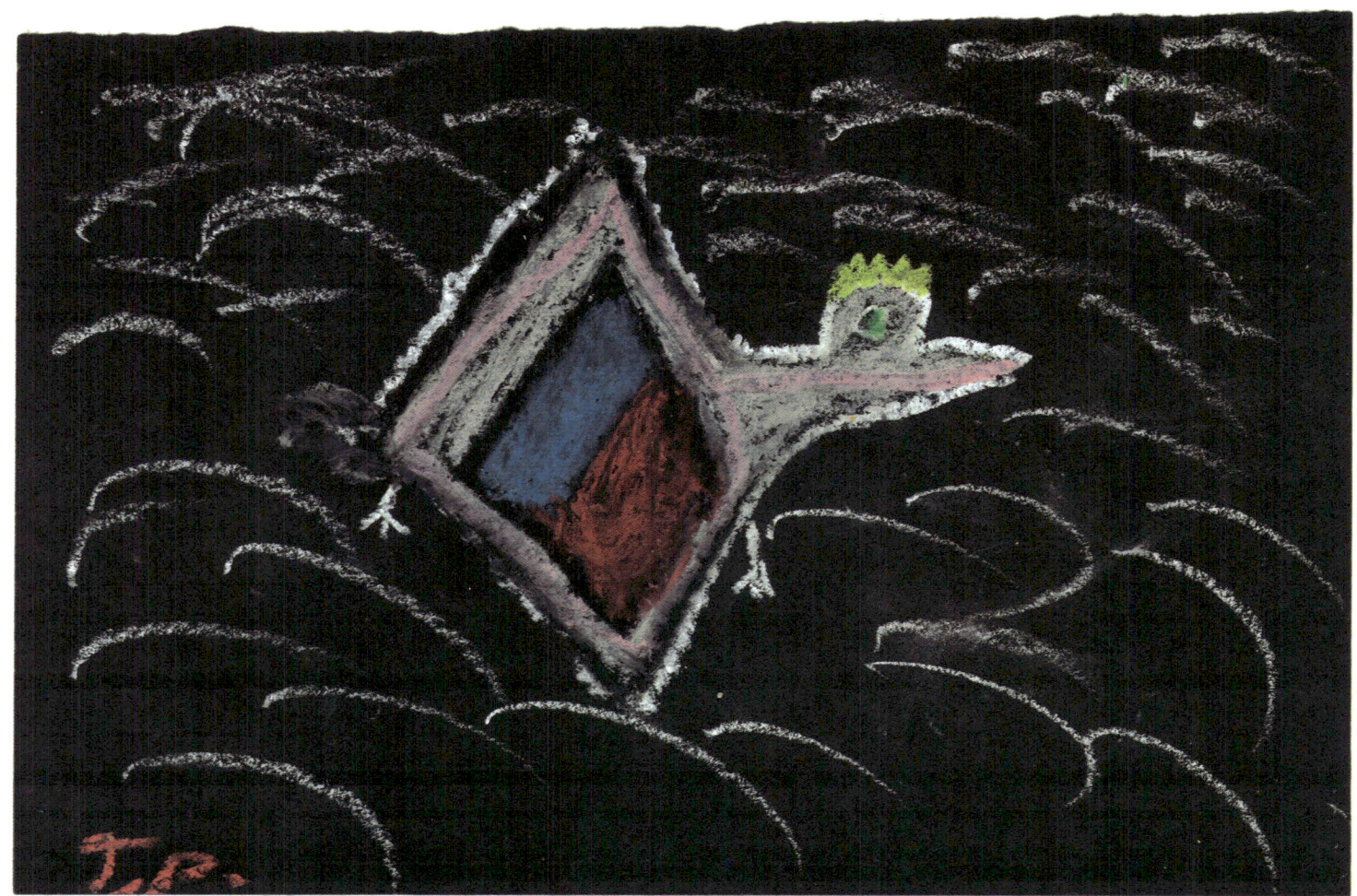

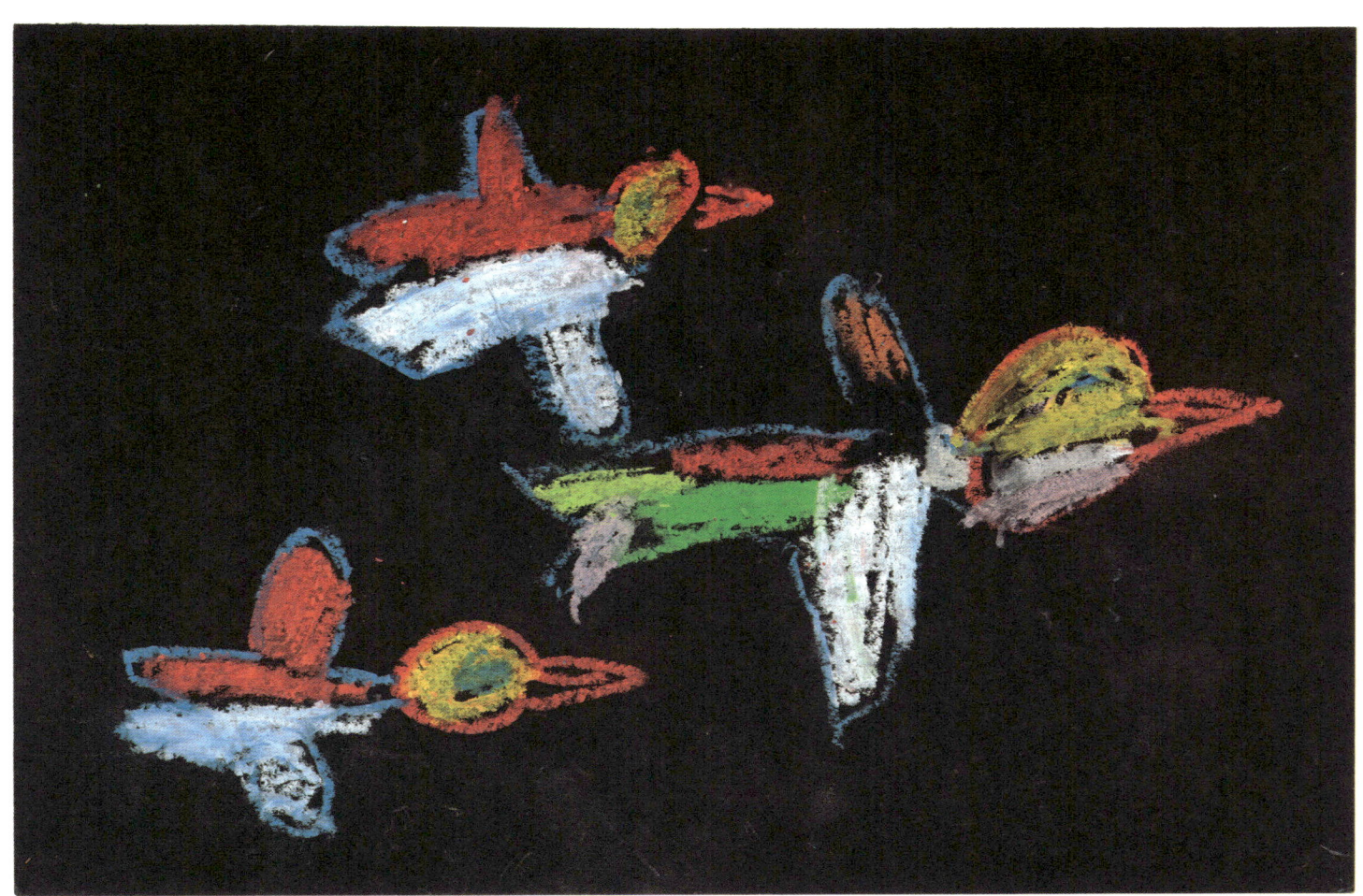

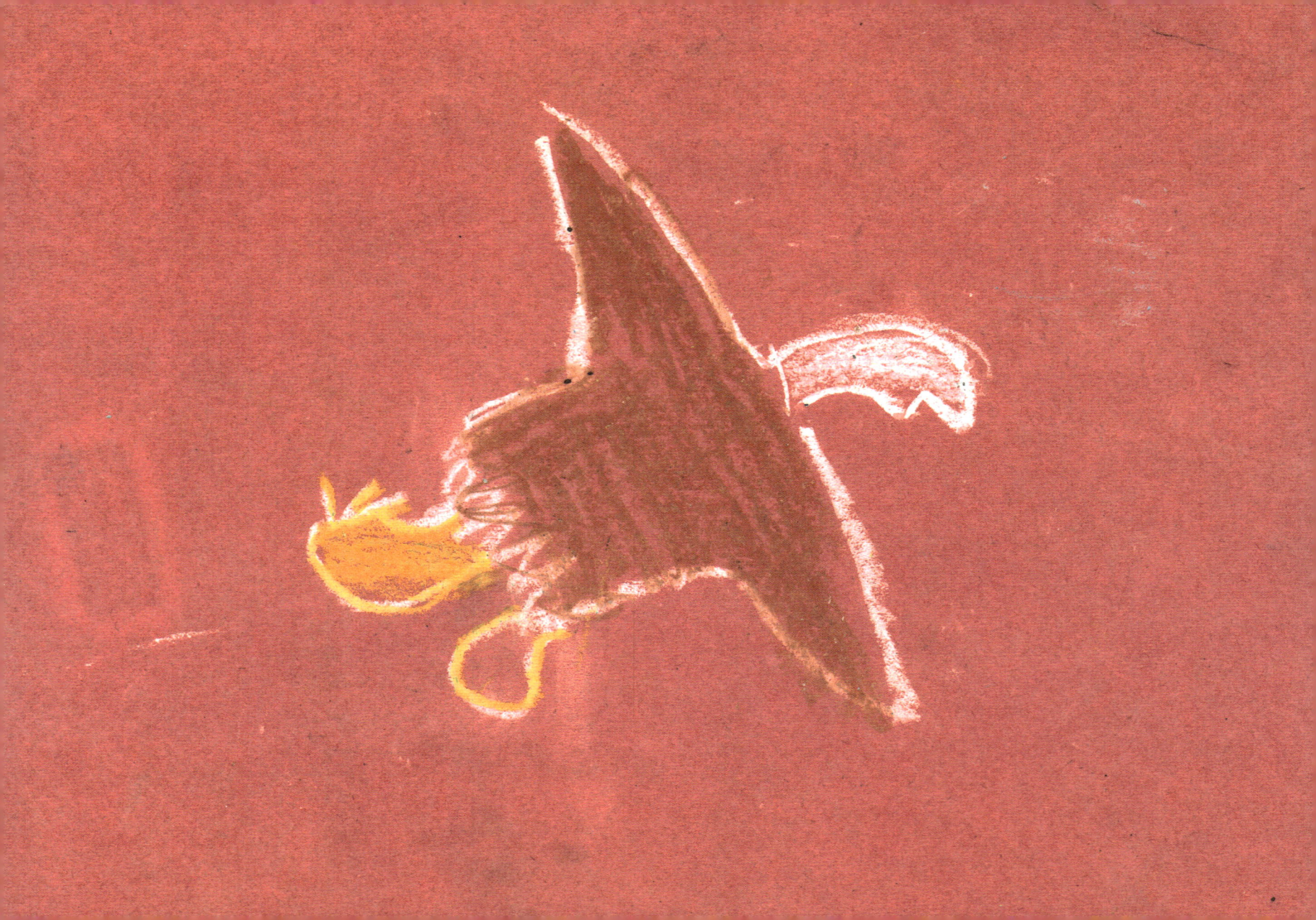

Birds of Imagining

*My bird moves swiftly
throughout the land.
It's very special.
It has a great home
of wonder.*
　　　　　—Ebony, age 11

*The bird of imagination
has to get born because if it
didn't get born, we wouldn't be
able to get it out of our minds.*
　　　　　—Jarrod, age 9

*This bird makes
everything come alive.
She makes dead flowers
become into alive flowers.*
　　　　　—Leola, age 7

*My bird comes out at night on a
full moon. He flies through the sky.
At night you can never see him.
He is in you.
His name is imagination.
He lives in a place
called heart brain body. It is in everyone.
Some adults think it is childish
but it will never leave you even if you hide it.*
　　　　　—Joel, age 10

*The shadow of the bird
of imagination is heavier
than a thought.*
　　　　　—Joelle, age 11

*My bird of imagination
can glow in the dark.*
　　　　　—Jasminda, age 7

The Bird of Imagining

There was a bird no one had ever seen before.
A bird whose feathers caught the colors
of light shining through them,
so that each feather
reflected the hues of all the days
and all the nights.

There was a bird no one had ever seen before.
A bird whose eyes could feel the time
of what had been and what will be –
and feeling the life of all this time,
could see inside and outside of what it saw.

There was a bird no one had ever seen before.
A bird whose wings gathered the air around them,
filling the weight of those wings with the breathing of
    creatures,
listening, in suspense, to other sounds.

There was a bird no one had ever seen before.
A bird whose voices were the words of dreams,
changing into the songs that brought the stars closer,
so they could have the warmth of their singing nearby.

There was a bird no one had ever seen before,
and it was – *ourselves,*
ready to be in the sky of our thoughts,

to be the dreaming of our night into day,
to be the speaking of our words into song,
to be the feet of our dance,
to be the music of our play.

There was a bird no one had ever seen before,
and it flew –
and nothing,
and no one,
was ever the same afterwards . . .

Artwork and Writings

Artwork

Front Jacket: Bianca 2nd Grade, Children's Workshop School • *Half-title:* Unsigned, 3rd/4th Grade, Central Park East #2 • *Page 7:* David, 1st/2nd Grade, Central Park East #1 • *Page 8:* Jessica, Kindergarten, Children's Workshop School • *Page 9:* Shunguke, 2nd Grade, Children's Workshop School • *Page 11:* Klay, Kindergarten, Children's Workshop School • *Page 12:* Jhon-Paul, Kindergarten, Children's Workshop School • *Page 13:* Do-Son, 5th Grade, Children's Workshop School • *Page 15:* Mantza, 1st Grade, Children's Workshop School • *Page 16:* Ben, 1st Grade, Children's Workshop School • *Page 17:* Unsigned, Central Park East #2 • *Page 19:* Tanaieo, 5th Grade, Children's Workshop School • *Page 20:* Jianna, 1st/2nd Grade, Central Park East #1 • *Page 21:* Yuga, 1st Grade, Children's Workshop School • *Page 23:* Tiffany, 1st/2nd Grade, Central Park East #1 • *Page 24:* Cady, Pre-K, Children's Workshop School • *Page 25:* Luis, Pre-K, Children's Workshop School • *Page 27:* Clair, Kindergarten, Children's Workshop School • *Page 28:* Jeremy, 1st Grade, Children's Workshop School • *Page 29:* Daniel, 5th Grade, Children's Workshop School • *Page 31:* Ashley, 1st Grade, Children's Workshop School • *Page 32:* Eric, Central Park East #2 • *Page 33:* Tene, 1st Grade, Children's Workshop School • *Page 35:* Teisha, 1st/2nd Grade, Central Park East #1 • *Page 36:* John Paul, 5th Grade, Children's Workshop School • *Page 37:* Brisitte, Kindergarten, Children's Workshop School • *Page 38:* Steven, Central Park East #2 *Back Jacket:* (left to right) Jessica, Kindergarten, Children's Workshop School • David, 1st/2nd Grade, Central Park East #1 • Jianna, 1st/2nd Grade, Central Park East #1 • Do-Son, 5th Grade, Children's Workshop School

Writings

Page 39: Ebony, 5th/6th Grade, River East School • Jarrod, 3rd/4th Grade, River East School • Leola, 1st/2nd Grade, Central Park East School #1 • Joel, 5th/6th Grade, River East School • Joelle, 5th/6th Grade, River East School Jasminda, 2nd Grade, Children's Workshop School • *Back Jacket:* Joel, 5th/6th Grade, River East School

A Note on the Artwork

The artwork in this book was created by children five through eleven years old in several New York City public schools, as part of The Touchstone Center's Thematic Residency Program, *The Flight of the Imagination*. These arts and education workshops were first given at the Central Park East School #1 and #2 and the River East School in the fall of 1989 through the spring of 1990. A second group of workshops took place at the Children's Workshop School during the spring of 1996.

Workshops were held once a week in classes ranging from pre-kindergarden to sixth grade, for a period of six to eight weeks. At the beginning of each series of workshops I read my poem, *The Bird of Imagining*, accompanied by Touchstone teacher-artist Gigi Alvaré, who accentuated various elements of the poem through movement and puppets she had created specifically for the poem. Our intent was to give children a metaphoric starting point to reflect upon the qualities of their own imaginations. Following our reading and performance, children were asked to draw with oil pastels on construction paper what they thought their birds of imagination looked like. After finishing their drawings, children were then encouraged to write down, or dictate to us, all the things their birds of imagining could do – and how they came to be. In subsequent workshops, using their original drawings and writings as guides, each child made a mask and wings out of paper and cardboard to represent their birds of imagining. These masks and wings were finally given flight when they were worn by the children in a series of outdoor events celebrating the marvel and uniqueness of each child's imagination.

Acknowledgments

Our deepest gratitude to the many children who participated in this project, in particular, those children whose art and writing is included in this book. We thank each one of you for sharing your unique vision of your bird of imagining – and for the continued inspiration of your expressiveness and genuine artistry.

We also want to thank the following teachers and staff who enthusiastically participated in and hosted *The Flight of the Imagination* project in their schools and classrooms: Idely Torres, Laurie Friedlander, Jill Olesker, and Esther Rosenfeld from Central Park East #2; Cordelia Castillo, Pam Cushing, and Jane Andreas from Central Park East #1; Sid Massey, Abby Lincoln, and Leslie Alexander from the River East School; and Gary Morston, Nicki Weiss, Norma Leutzinger, Jim Shoaf, Debbie Friedland, Danette Lebron, Maria Velez-Clarke, and Jean Finnerty from the Children's Workshop School.

Without the sensitive and inventive teaching of my associate, Gigi Alvaré, this project would not have come to life as it did. My thanks to her – and my appreciation for her steadfastness throughout our working partnership.

The Touchstone Center is most grateful for the generous support of the following funders, who made this project possible: New York State Council on the Arts, Chase Manhattan Bank, District 4 of the New York City Board of Education, Parents' Association of Central Park East #2, Con Edison, Aaron Diamond Foundation, The New York Times Company Foundation, Frances Lewis Trust, and the Parents' Association of the Children's Workshop School.

The Touchstone Center for Children

is a nonprofit educational organization based in New York City. Since its founding in 1969, the Center has created a variety of interdisciplinary arts programs in public schools that explore the role of the imagination as pivotal to all learning. The Center's work has concentrated on developing the use of elemental themes and images in order to encourage both children and adults to express, through different expressive mediums, their innate relationship to the natural world. With its artist residencies in schools, publications, exhibitions, theatre productions, and workshops and seminars for educators, the Center has been committed to sustaining the importance of the imaginative process as a means of deepening individual and collective understanding.

*

A portion of the proceeds from sales of this book will be donated to the arts and education programs of the Children's Workshop School, the River East School, and Central Park East #1 and #2.

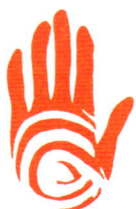